Rosa Parks Sits Down

SRA

Columbus, OH

Cover © Time & Life Pictures / Getty Images; **3** © Comstock Images / Alamy;
4 © Bettmann / Corbis; **5** © Time & Life Pictures / Getty Images;
6 (tl) © Bettmann / Corbis; **6** (bl) © Bettmann / Corbis; **6** (br) © Getty Images;
7 © Time Life Pictures / Getty Images; **8** © Getty Images; **9** (t) © AP Wide
World Photos; **9** (bl) © AP Wide World Photos; **10** © Time & Life Pictures /
Getty Images; **11** © Time & Life Pictures / Getty Images.

SRAonline.com

 SRA

Copyright © 2008 by SRA/McGraw-Hill.

All rights reserved. No part of this publication may be
reproduced or distributed in any form or by any means,
or stored in a database or retrieval system, without the
prior written consent of The McGraw-Hill Companies,
Inc., including, but not limited to, network storage or
transmission, or broadcast for distance learning.
An Open Court Curriculum.

Printed in China.

Send all inquiries to this address:
SRA/McGraw-Hill
4400 Easton Commons
Columbus, OH 43219

ISBN: 978-0-07-606647-6
MHID: 0-07-606647-9

1 2 3 4 5 6 7 8 9 NOR 13 12 11 10 09 08 07

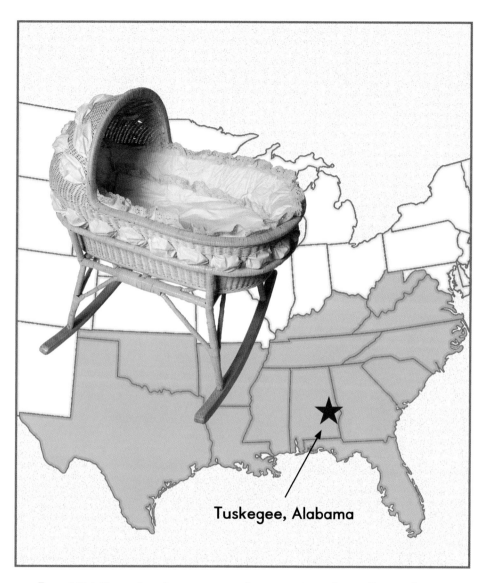

Tuskegee, Alabama

In 1913 a baby was born in the South. Her name was Rosa Parks. One day she would be famous.

Parks grew up on a farm. At age eleven, she went to a school in the city. Think of her excitement!

Parks left school when her grandmother got sick. Parks wanted to help her. But she did not give up on school. She finished at age twenty-one.

In the South, African Americans had to follow many laws. Usually these laws kept them away from white people. Parks wanted to make things fairer.

There were laws about riding a bus.
Parks had more than one problem with
these laws.

In 1955 Parks had a big problem on a bus. A white man wanted her seat. She said no. She clenched her jaw and waited.

The police came.
Parks must have been
trembling with fear.
But she did not give in.
They took her to jail.

Three days later most black people in the city stopped riding buses. For more than a year they walked everywhere.

Then the laws were changed. What a thrill for Rosa Parks! She had helped make thing more fair.

Vocabulary

excitement (ik sīt´ mənt) (page 4) *n.* A mood or feeling of high interest or energy; delight; joy.

usually (ū´ zhōō əl ē) (page 6) *adv.* Most of the time.

problem (prob´ ləm) (page 7) *n.* A personal difficulty; a tricky or uncomfortable situation.

clenched (klencht) (page 8) *v.* Past tense of **clench:** To close tightly.

trembling (trem´ bəl ing) (page 9) A form of the verb **tremble:** To shake.

thrill (thril) (page 11) *n.* A feeling of excitement.

Comprehension Focus: Cause and Effect

1. Why did Rosa leave school?
2. Why did black people in Rosa Parks's city stop riding buses?